JAMEST(

THE CONTEMPORARY READER

VOLUME 3, NUMBER 3

Mc Graw Hill **Glencoe McGraw-Hill**

New York, New York   Columbus, Ohio   Chicago, Illinois   Peoria, Illinois   Woodland Hills, California

JAMESTOWN EDUCATION

Glencoe/McGraw-Hill

A Division of The **McGraw·Hill** Companies

Send all inquiries to:
Glencoe/McGraw-Hill
8787 Orion Place
Columbus, OH 43240-4027

ISBN: 0-07-827362-5

Printed in the United States of America

1 2 3 4 5 6 7 8 9 10 113 09 08 07 06 05 04 03

CONTENTS

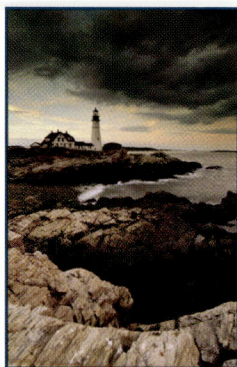

Pronunciation Key

ă	m**a**t	o͞o	f**oo**d
ā	d**a**te	o͝o	l**oo**k
â	b**a**re	ŭ	dr**u**m
ä	f**a**ther	yo͞o	c**u**te
ĕ	w**e**t	û	f**u**r
ē	s**ee**	*th*	**th**en
ĭ	t**i**p	th	**th**in
ī	**i**ce	hw	**wh**ich
î	p**ie**rce	zh	u**s**ual
ŏ	h**o**t	ə	**a**lone
ō	n**o**		op**e**n
ô	l**a**w		pen**c**il
oi	b**oi**l		lem**o**n
ou	l**ou**d		camp**u**s

A late-winter storm paralyzed New York City in March of 1888. This photo shows snow blanketing a row of apartment buildings near Trinity Church.

The Storm That Changed New York City

How did disaster lead to progress in New York City?

1   The calendar read March 11, 1888. Spring was definitely on the way. The weather was warm and rainy. In New York City, people wore their spring clothes. The weather forecast for the next day was for fair skies, but the weather forecast was wrong. Dead wrong.

The Storm Begins

2   In the evening, the rain turned to snow. By morning, the wind had started to howl and the temperature had plummeted[1] to near zero. The city woke up to find almost a foot of snow on the ground, with more falling by the minute.

3   Most people tried to get to work anyway. In those days, if you failed to get to work—for any

---

[1] plummeted: plunged; fell straight down

reason—someone else would be hired to take your place that very day. Also, working people could not afford to lose a day's pay. Losing that pay meant their families might not eat.

4   However, it was almost impossible to move about in the streets of New York City that morning. Only the strongest walkers could battle the wind and the snow. The streets were clogged with carts that had gotten stuck in the snow and been left behind. The horses couldn't get through the deep drifts to pull the snowplows. The streetcars[2] couldn't stay on the tracks.

5   The wind was so strong that signs and pieces of buildings were torn off and fell into the streets. Telegraph poles blew over, and the wires hung down or broke. The Blizzard of 1888 had begun.

What Is a Blizzard?

6   A blizzard is more than a common snowstorm. In addition to snow, a blizzard also has high winds and very cold temperatures. In the 1888 blizzard the winds blew up to 80 miles per hour. The temperature dropped so low that it set a record that has never been broken.

7   In the American Midwest, where the land is flat and there are few trees, people had become

---

[2] streetcar: a bus-like vehicle on rails that carries passengers on city streets

Blizzards disrupted all city services. Many power lines broke under the weight of ice and snow.

used to blizzards. But these Easterners didn't know what had hit them. The blizzard did not let up for 72 hours. It covered Pennsylvania, New Jersey, New York, and most of New England, dropping a huge amount of snow. In fact, some places were buried under an astounding amount of snow—more than four feet!

8   Even worse than the snow was the wind. It pushed the snow into drifts up to 40 feet high. The wind kept moving the snow so that the streets couldn't be cleared. One side of a street might be bare, and the other side covered with a 20-foot drift.

9   Wind forced the fine snow under doors and windows. Outside, it froze ice onto pedestrians' faces and clothing. People trying to walk in the thick snowfall couldn't see where they were going, and the air was so full of blowing snow that they couldn't breathe. Some people became so exhausted that they just fell down where they were and were quickly covered by the blowing snow.

10   Trains were stopped on their tracks, and they weren't dug out for 48 hours. Ships on the ocean could not be saved from the huge waves because no one could see the waves in the blowing snow!

Snow blown by high winds blinded pedestrians. It also buried many who were blown down or who could not continue.

New York City and the Blizzard

11 More than 400 people died in the Blizzard of 1888. About 200 of these deaths were in New York City alone. New Yorkers found themselves in dire straits[3] for several reasons. For example, in those days, most homes did not have refrigerators, so people had to shop for food every day. The markets were soon empty, however, and people had no food at all in their houses. The price of milk shot up from two cents a quart to 15 cents—if it was available at all.

12 People were also extremely cold. After all, it was spring, and the average household had used up all the coal in its coal bin. Without coal to fuel their furnaces, New Yorkers had no way to keep warm.

13 Transportation into and out of the city was a major problem. People who had managed to get to work on Monday morning soon discovered that they couldn't get home. No bridges had been built in New York City yet, so many city workers had to commute[4] by ferry boat. But the boats couldn't fight the high winds and the ice. Commuters crammed into the ferry buildings or stood outside all night in the blizzard. An unlucky few tried to walk across the river on the

---

[3] dire straits: deep trouble; crisis
[4] commute: to travel back and forth regularly, as between a city and a suburb

ice, but when the ice broke, they were swept down the river.

14   The biggest city in the United States was cut off from the rest of the world. All the telegraph wires were down. Radios had not been invented yet, so there was no news from the outside world for three days.

Cleaning Up After the Blizzard

15   At last, on March 14, the blizzard ended, and it was time to shovel out. In those days, all shoveling had to be done by hand. Clearing a sidewalk 100 feet long and five feet wide with 15 inches of snow on it meant lifting two *tons* of snow! Snow had to be shoveled into carts and hauled to the river. The city hired hundreds of workers to shovel. Officials estimated that they filled 11.5 million carts with snow just to clear one neighborhood. Some people tried building fires to melt the snow. But the melting snow simply made puddles that froze again into slippery sheets of ice.

16   It took a long time to get rid of the snow. Seven weeks later, on April 29, the temperature in New York City hit 100 degrees. As city dwellers dealt with the heat, they were reminded of the storm by the 14 inches of snow still left on the ground!

17   The people of New York City were determined never to suffer a disaster like that

Workers shovel snow into horse-drawn carts. The snow was dumped into the East River.

again. They knew that they had no control over the weather, but they could change the way the city operated. For that reason, almost as soon as the snow was gone, work crews started to dig. They buried all the telegraph wires so the wires couldn't fall. Never again would the city be cut off from the news of the world.

18   The city also began to switch over to electric streetcars. An electric streetcar could push a plow in deep snow, thereby clearing the snow more easily and more quickly than a horse-drawn plow

could. Also, streetcars would never get so cold and tired that they would collapse and die, a constant worry with horses. From then on no more elevated[5] trains were built. Instead, the city started planning a subway so that trains could run underground, away from the weather. New York City began to look the way it does today.

19 Today, with better weather forecasts, we are not usually caught off guard by dangerous storms. And with powerful snowplows to remove the snow, we have an easier time digging out. But if a storm as terrible as the Blizzard of 1888 ever came along again, we would still have a hard time dealing with it! ◆

---

[5] elevated: raised; running on tracks built over city streets

QUESTIONS

1. During which month did the Blizzard of 1888 happen?
2. What are some differences between a snowstorm and a blizzard?
3. Why was New York City cut off from news of the world during the blizzard?
4. How did New York City clear the snow from its streets?
5. Name two changes that New Yorkers made to protect their city against future snow disasters.

An eager sled dog team hurries toward the starting line
to begin the annual Iditarod race across Alaska.

Iditarod:
the
Last Great Race

What could inspire people to race 1,200 miles across Alaska in the dead of winter?

1   Imagine climbing aboard a sled behind a pack of excited dogs. Imagine racing day and night for weeks across snow, ice, frozen rivers, and dangerous mountains. Some brave folks in Alaska do more than use their imaginations. They actually risk their safety in a famous race every March. The race is the Iditarod [ī dǐt´ə rŏd] Trail Sled Dog Race, also known as the Last Great Race. Only one racer can come in first and win the prize. But every finisher wins the respect of the other racers and of fans around the world.

2   The Iditarod Trail leads from Anchorage through the Alaskan wilderness to Nome. It crosses forests, tundra,[1] and mountain ranges. A race this long over such dangerous terrain[2] brings out the best in both humans and animals.

---

[1] tundra: a huge area of flat land in very cold parts of the world with no trees and a layer of permanently frozen soil under the surface

[2] terrain: ground; land

11

The History of the Race

3   During Alaska's Centennial in 1967, planners wanted to find an activity that called to mind Alaska's rough-and-ready past. They hit upon the idea of having a grand dogsled race. After all, dogsleds were the major way of getting around Alaska until the airplane became common.

4   But where would they have the race? The planners decided to use the rugged Iditarod Trail. This nearly 1,200-mile trail between Anchorage and Nome was famous for two reasons. First, it was a trail that had been central to the lives of Alaskans for decades. Second, there was an exciting story of danger and courage connected with it.

A Lifeline to the Outside

5   The history of Alaska is closely connected to the search for gold. In fact, many of the towns in Alaska were founded during the great gold rushes from the 1880s to the 1920s. During the summer, towns such as Nome could be reached by steamboats. But during the winter, all ocean and river traffic stopped. The only way to get in and out of these northern towns was by dogsled. In 1910 the federal government created the Iditarod Trail for dogsled teams. Teams of 20 or more dogs would pull 1,000-pound freight sleds carrying mail, food, and other supplies into the towns. They would carry mail and gold out. A

The rugged conditions on the Iditarod trail challenge both musher and dogs.

round-trip journey from Anchorage to Nome could take almost six weeks. For decades[3] many people who lived in Alaska depended on these dogsleds to supply them with what they needed until the next spring.

A Race Against Death

6   In the winter of 1925, a serious illness, diphtheria[4] [dĭf thîr´ē ə], broke out in the isolated town of Nome. Alaskans knew that diphtheria could spread and kill quickly.

---

[3] decade: a period of 10 years

[4] diphtheria: a highly contagious disease that causes a sore throat, high fever, and the formation of material in the throat that may block air passages and affect breathing

Balto, a lead sled dog, was one of the heroes who saved the city of Nome from an epidemic in early 1925. He poses for this photo with sledder Gunnar Kasson in July of that year.

Children, especially, were at risk. Nome needed a serum[5] to fight the disease. The nearest serum supply was in Anchorage. The planes that flew to Nome during the summer were in storage. And the weather was so bad that flying posed a terrible risk.

7   The governor of Alaska decided to use a dogsled relay along the Iditarod Trail to take the medicine from Anchorage to Nome. The serum was wrapped in a heavy quilt and put aboard a train in Anchorage. The train tracks ended at Nenana [nə nä´nä], about 250 miles north of Anchorage.

8   At Nenana a musher, or dogsled driver, picked up the package. Then one brave musher-and-dog team after the other took the serum farther and farther. The trip was brutal. Temperatures

---

[5] serum: a thin, clear liquid in blood. Serum taken from an animal that has already had a disease can be used to protect humans from getting the disease

reached 50 degrees below zero, blinding snow fell, and strong winds blew. But the mushers continued. Finally, a team led by a dog named Balto arrived in downtown Nome. The children were saved.

The Race Today

9   Today, men and women from all over the world race over the Iditarod Trail and remember the past. Not just anyone is allowed to race, however. Mushers and their teams must show they are ready for this punishing test. No one

A dogsled team scrambles uphill at Rainy Pass in the Alaska Range.

wants to see people or dogs in trouble on the trail. So mushers must prove themselves in at least two other dogsled races before they compete here.

10   Just before the race, mushers outfit themselves with lightweight sleds, food, medicine, and fuel for the trail. They send extra food and supplies to a series of roadhouses along the trail. But the most important items the racers need are good sled dogs.

11   Race rules permit no more than 16 dogs per team. The dogs a racer begins with are the same ones that cross the finish line. No additions or substitutions may be made. If a dog gets sick or injured, it drops out. The rest of the team usually keeps going. The dogs are hooked together in pairs on a "gangline," a central rope. The team can stretch to about 80 feet in length, from lead dog to sled.

12   The musher stands at the back of the sled. He or she never uses reins to control the dogs. All commands are given by voice. The lead dog hears and obeys the commands. The rest of the team follow. On the trail the musher hardly ever needs to shout commands. The dogs can follow the trail in silence for hours. When mushers need to communicate with their dogs, they use special words. To start the team, the musher might say, "Hike" or "Let's go!" Calls of "gee" or "haw" tell the dogs to turn right or left. As you might guess, "whoa" tells dogs to stop. Some mushers, such as

Four-time Iditarod winner Susan Butcher and her sled dogs take a break during a training run.

four-time winner Susan Butcher, use a personal code with their dogs. Susan uses a kissing sound to tell the dogs to run. Her whistle tells them to run even faster, in a short sprint.

13   The race begins on the first Saturday in March. It starts in Anchorage in even-numbered years and in Nome in odd-numbered years. Over the next two, three, or even four weeks, the teams will race day and night. They must take one 24-hour rest period and two 8-hour rest periods. Otherwise, they may race whenever they have the energy. To keep the

dogs' paws safe, mushers outfit them with cloth booties. To make sure the dogs stay healthy, veterinarians examine them at checkpoints along the trail. Between checkpoints and roadhouses, mushers and their teams are entirely on their own in often dangerous conditions. Race officials do try to lessen the perils that mushers face. They ask volunteers to drive snowmobiles down the trail a few hours ahead of the leader to make sure that the trail is passable and as free of problems as possible.

And the Winner Is . . .

14   The people celebrate when the winner crosses the finish line on Front Street. They don't care what time of day or night this happens. A fire siren is sounded and crowds run out to greet the winner. Teams straggle in for days after the winner arrives. Every time another racer comes in, the fire siren is sounded again, and a crowd gathers around the tired musher. The fastest that anyone has ever finished the race is nine days and about one hour. The longest time any team has ever taken to finish the race is 32 days and about 15 hours.

15   Alaskans appreciate the courage it takes to travel the Iditarod Trail. In the past, when people knew a team was on the trail, they lit lanterns to lead the musher to food and a place to rest. Now, at the beginning of each Iditarod race, a

lantern is lit in Nome. It stays lit until the last musher crosses the finish line. That musher gets a special prize called the Red Lantern Award. Then the light is put out—until the next March, that is—when the fun starts all over again. ◆

QUESTIONS

1. Which two cities are on either end of the Iditarod Trail?
2. What items did mushers carry to inland towns during the early 1900s? What did they carry away?
3. Why were mushers in such a hurry to get to Nome during the winter of 1925?
4. Name and explain two commands a musher gives his or her dogs.
5. What measures help sled dogs stay safe and healthy during the race?
6. What award is given to the last finisher in the Iditarod Trail Sled Dog Race?

A Monument to America

*How did Gutzon Borglum honor
his beloved country?*

1 Gutzon Borglum [go͞ot´sŭn bôr´glŭm] was born
in Idaho in 1867. He grew up on the frontier
and got used to its vast open spaces. To him, the
very *bigness* of the land seemed to offer endless
choices. The son of a Danish immigrant,
Borglum loved America deeply. Someday, he
thought, he would do something great to honor
his homeland.

The huge faces carved into Mount Rushmore are a tribute to
four American presidents. In this photo, two construction
workers are carving a single eye on one face.

21

Borglum the Sculptor

2 When still a young man, Borglum decided to become an artist. In the 1890s he traveled to Paris, France, to study art. There he met the famous sculptor[1] Auguste Rodin [ō gōōst´ rō dăn´]. (Rodin's best-known work is *The Thinker*.) The sculptor showed him how to use light in a new way. Borglum learned that light reflecting off of perfectly cut rock could make the eyes of a statue seem alive. Borglum would use what he learned in France throughout his life as a sculptor.

3   Borglum returned home in 1901 and immediately began to sculpt. Some of his works became quite popular with the American public. Abraham Lincoln was one of his favorite subjects. Borglum created a marble bust[2] of Lincoln that is displayed in the Capitol in Washington, D.C. Another of his sculptures of Lincoln can still be viewed in Newark, New Jersey. It is called "the children's Lincoln" because boys and girls often crawl onto Lincoln's roomy lap.

---

[1] sculptor: an artist who makes or carves figures using materials such as stone, clay, or marble

[2] bust: a sculpture that shows the head and upper chest of a person

**Crews labored on the project from 1927 to 1941.
Above, stonecutters climb George Washington's nose.**

Dreaming Big

4   Borglum wanted to do something really
    important. He believed that the power of
    America came from its ability to think big
    thoughts and to dare great deeds. He wanted his
    art to communicate that idea. In 1923 he got the
    chance he had been waiting for. Duane
    Robinson, a state official in South Dakota,

contacted him. Robinson was looking for someone to carve a monument into the side of a mountain in the Black Hills. He thought Borglum was the man for the job. At first, Robinson suggested that Borglum carve heroes of the Old West, such as Red Cloud, Sacagawea, and Jim Bridger.

Workers perched on scaffolding cut away tons of stone to shape the faces.

5   Borglum jumped at the chance to carve such a large monument. However, he didn't want to carve local heroes. Instead, he wanted to carve a true *national* monument. So Borglum suggested that he carve the heads of two presidents, Abraham Lincoln and George Washington. Later, he would add Thomas Jefferson and Theodore Roosevelt to his design. Robinson and others agreed with Borglum's ideas.

6   The first site that Robinson chose proved to be unsuitable. The site finally picked for the sculpture was Mount Rushmore. Not everyone was pleased with this choice. The Sioux nation protested because they believe the area to be sacred. Since the Black Hills area had been deeded to them in 1868, they didn't feel it was right to allow the sculpture to be carved there. Others felt that the natural beauty of the mountain would be ruined by the work. Those who wanted the sculpture carved on Mount Rushmore won out, however, and work was begun.

A Bold Plan

7   It was a bold plan, but Borglum was a bold man who was equal to the task. "Let us place there, carved high, as close to heaven as we can, our leaders," he said.

8   Borglum wanted Americans to remember these great men. His sculpture would show "what

manner[3] of men they were." He wanted people to look at the carvings "until the wind and rain alone shall wear them away."

Rock Carving

9 The task was enormous. First, Borglum carved four five-foot-high heads to serve as models. Each head on the actual monument would be 60 feet high, so every inch in the models represented one foot in the sculpture. The heads would have to be carved carefully out of the rocky face of Mount Rushmore. Work on the mountain finally began in August 1927.

10 Painters create their art by adding color to a blank canvas. But many sculptors do not add; instead, they take away. The art of sculpting is sometimes in the removal of just the right material. In a sense, Lincoln and the other three presidents were already locked up in the rock. Borglum's job was to free them.

11 At first, Borglum refused to use dynamite. One mistake could ruin the cliff. The granite was just too hard, however, so he soon changed his mind. Borglum allowed workers to set off blasts of dynamite, but he supervised their work carefully.

12 The next task was to shape the faces. Miners, not artists, were recruited to do this work.

---

[3] manner: kind; sort

The presidents' images from left to right are George Washington, Thomas Jefferson, Theodore Roosevelt, and Abraham Lincoln.

Borglum gave them detailed instructions about where to cut away rock. They climbed onto long swing seats that were suspended from the mountaintop and lowered into the proper positions. Borglum's crew, and sometimes he himself, drilled away at the mountain's face. They also used hammers and chisels to smooth the granite stone. Slowly, the faces of the four presidents emerged.

13   Just two years into the project, Borglum's supply of funds from private donations ran out.

The faces on Mt. Rushmore can be seen from miles away, even without the use of high-powered binoculars.

At that point the federal government stepped in to fund the project. Finally, in 1941, the massive work of art was finished. The job had taken 14 years and had cost just under $1 million. Sadly, Gutzon Borglum died before the work was finished. His son, Lincoln, stepped in to complete the job for him.

Mount Rushmore Today

14   Mount Rushmore is now South Dakota's number one attraction. Each year nearly three million tourists come to see it. As many as 20,000 come in a single day.

15   Most visitors agree it is worth the trip. Mount Rushmore is an awesome sight. In the right light, the 60-foot heads seem almost alive. As one local person said, "You feel those four men looking right at you."

16   Gutzon Borglum would have been proud to hear that. But he would have liked the words of Jim Popovich of the National Park Service even more. "This isn't a monument to presidents," Popovich said. "It's a monument to America." ◆

Q U E S T I O N S

1. Where did Gutzon Borglum grow up?
2. Why did Borglum want to carve the faces of the four presidents, not heroes of the Old West, on Mount Rushmore?
3. In what way is sculpting different from painting?
4. How long did it take to create the Mount Rushmore monument?
5. Why do you suppose Borglum named his son Lincoln?

The Federal Reserve Bank in New York City, one of 12 in the system, houses gold bars worth billions of dollars.

THREE CHEER$ for the FED!

*Why is the
Federal Reserve System so important to
our nation's money?*

1   You probably know that managing your family's
money is a big job. But just imagine trying to
manage the money for an entire country! In 1913
the United States created a special agency to
control the nation's money supply. It is called the
Federal Reserve System. Today, the Fed, as the
system is nicknamed, has these jobs:
- storing a large supply of gold for safekeeping
- setting up rules for the smaller U.S. banks
- keeping track of transfers between U.S. banks and
  between the United States and other countries

- keeping track of money paid by checks
- ordering the U.S. Treasury's Bureau of Engraving and Printing to make new currency[1] and to distribute the currency
- working with the Secret Service to guard against the making and circulation of fake money

Keeping Gold Safe

2 Deep in the basement of the Federal Reserve Bank in New York City is a treasure. Behind a 90-ton steel door sits $70 billion worth of gold stored as gold bars. The gold belongs to countries all around the world. Each country's gold bars are kept in a separate room or pile. Every 28-pound gold bar is worth more than $100,000. When a country buys or sells gold to another nation, Fed workers place the correct number of bars on a small cart and then pull the cart from the selling country's room to the buying country's room. In this way, transactions worth billions of dollars are handled quietly and simply.

[1] currency: money

Bills are printed 24 hours a day by the Bureau of Engraving and Printing.

Making the Rules

3   Not everything the Fed does is so simple. In fact, its major job is unbelievably complex.[2] The Fed pays close attention to the nation's economy and the way the country uses its resources. The goal of the Fed is to make sure the economy stays healthy. After all, a healthy economy makes it possible for the nation's people to have the things they need. Achieving that goal takes the cooperation of all the banks in the country. One of the tasks of the Fed is to decide what amount banks should charge each other to borrow money. The Fed also makes rules about how much money banks must keep in a central place.

_____

[2] complex: not simple; made up of many related parts

These rules affect the average American in a variety of ways. For example, they determine how much it costs to borrow money for house and car loans.

Transferring Money

4   Every day, banks and companies need to pay each other. Sometimes millions of dollars change hands at one time. It would be foolish for buyers to carry piles of bills to sellers, so the Fed makes the transaction easy. Computers at the Fed's Network Command Center transfer money very quickly. The computers subtract money from one account and add it to another. These transfers are not only fast—they are also cheap and safe. About $2.1 trillion moves through the center every day.

Every bank needs cash on hand for daily operations. These bundles of bills are being readied for transfer.

Keeping Track of Checks

5   A check is an order to a bank to
pay a certain amount of
money. Americans pay many
of their debts by check. It is
the Fed's job to make sure that
all of the people who are owed
money receive it. Federal Reserve banks have
machines that can scan about 1,800 checks per
minute. In one day, about six million checks
worth more than $10 billion can pass through
these machines. Each machine sorts the checks
by bank. Then computers take money from one
bank's account and give it to another bank.
Someday these transfers may be done only by
computer, without written checks.

Making Money

6   The Fed is in charge of making sure there are
enough paper money bills available for public use.
The Fed does not make the bills itself. Instead, it
tells the Bureau of Engraving and Printing how
many new or replacement bills are needed. Under
orders from the Fed, the Bureau of Engraving and
Printing produces bills 24 hours a day.

7   Making money is a long process. It begins at
the mill that makes the paper for the bills. First,
cotton and linen rags are loaded into a huge
boiler. The rags are cleaned and cooked for
25 hours. The cooking breaks the rags down

into a mushy pulp.[3] After harsh chemicals are added to the pulp, the mixture is spread on a mesh screen. Any remaining liquid drains through the screen. The pulp mix undergoes a second cooking, this time with bleach added. Next it is put into a press, and the water is squeezed out. The pulp is then cut into sheets. While it is still damp, security features are added.

8   Security features make it hard to copy the money that will be made from the pulp. Using a secret process, workers place a watermark on the pulp every six inches. A watermark is a picture or design that is stamped into paper. It can be seen only when you hold the paper up to light. On U.S. bills, the watermark is a shadow image of the person pictured on the front of the bill. The watermark is important in bill making because it cannot be photocopied.

9   In another secret process, plastic security strips are embedded[4] into the pulp. The security strip is different for each kind of bill. For example, the strip for a $20 bill bears these words: *USA TWENTY.* The letters are printed so that they can be read from either side. The strip in a $20 bill glows green under ultraviolet light. Only a few people in the world know how the strip is put into the pulp.

---

[3] pulp: a soft, wet mass of material
[4] embedded: fixed or enclosed within something

The Federal Reserve works with the U.S. Treasury to distribute money to banks. U.S. currency includes both bills and coins such as the Sacajawea dollar.

10   The pulp then travels through 25 dryers to become real paper. It is put through several tests. For example, to test the paper's strength, a sample is folded and unfolded 8,000 times. Paper that passes the tests is wound into rolls. The rolls are sent to the Bureau of Engraving and Printing, where each roll is put onto a huge printing machine. The printer can turn out 38 million bills in one day. It prints the backs of the bills first, in green ink. Then, after the green ink dries—in about 24 to 48 hours—it prints the fronts in black ink.

11   The printing process adds two more security features. Printers use a special ink that seems to change colors when the bill is viewed from different angles. To see this special feature for yourself, look at the numeral 20 on the lower right

side of a $20 bill. If you look at the bill directly, the numeral appears green. When you tilt the bill, the numeral changes to black. Another security feature is microprinting. Some lines on the bill are made up of tiny print. These letters are so small that they can be seen clearly only with a magnifying glass. They cannot be copied clearly; copiers smudge and blur them. To see microprinting, look closely at the lines inside the numeral 20 on the lower left side of a $20 bill. You will see that the lines are made up of tiny letters.

12   Each bill is given its own serial number printed in two places on the front of the bill. Finally, the bills receive the seals of the Federal Reserve and the U.S. Treasury. They are then ready to be distributed by Federal Reserve banks.

Fighting Fakes

13   Even with all of these safeguards, some people still make counterfeit[5] [koun´tər fĭt] bills. In fact, about $40 million in fake bills is passed every year in the United States. In cooperation with the Fed, the Secret Service keeps track of all of the fake bills that are found. Agents enter details about each one into a computer. Then they try to match new bills they find with old counterfeit

---

[5] counterfeit: not real; made to imitate something and fool people

bills on file. Sometimes they can track these bills to a certain place or person. In fact, in 1999 the Secret Service arrested nearly 4,000 counterfeiters.

14   The Federal Reserve System affects our lives every day. It works behind the scenes to make sure that the economy thrives, that the money supply is plentiful, and that the bills we use are genuine. Three cheers for the Fed! ◆

Q U E S T I O N S

1. When was the Federal Reserve System created?
2. Name two jobs of the Fed.
3. What is kept in the basement of the New York Federal Reserve Bank?
4. Name two security features on each bill.
5. What is a watermark, and why is it used?
6. Which agency is in charge of tracking down counterfeit bills?

Turtles in Trouble

Is it too late to save the sea turtles?

1   Sea turtles are prehistoric creatures that have survived for 175 million years. But how many will be around in 50 years? All eight kinds of sea turtles are in trouble today. Seven of the eight are considered endangered,[1] and the other type is threatened.[2] Efforts are being made to help sea turtles survive, but it is an uphill battle. If we are not careful, these magnificent creatures could soon be gone forever.

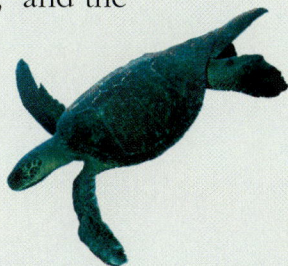

---

[1] endangered: referring to animals in immediate danger of dying out

[2] threatened: referring to animals that are plentiful in certain places but decreasing in number worldwide

Sea turtles, including this green turtle hatchling, are at risk.

41

From Largest to Smallest

2 Sea turtles are large, impressive animals. The largest of all is the leatherback. Leatherbacks are huge. An adult may weigh up to 2,000 pounds! The leatherback gets its name from the strange skin on its back. Whereas other turtles have shells, the leatherback has a soft, almost rubbery covering of skin.

3 The smallest sea turtle is the olive ridley. It weighs a mere 75 pounds. In between these two extremes fall the six other types of turtles. The green turtle and the loggerhead both weigh more than 200 pounds; the hawksbill, black, and flatback turtles weigh 100 to 200 pounds. The Kemp's ridley weighs in at just under 100 pounds.

4 Sea turtles span the globe and can be found in all warm-water oceans. Most swim in the Atlantic and Pacific oceans, around North America, Central America, and South America. The flatback, however, is found only in the waters off northern Australia.

5 Sea turtles feed on other marine[3] life. Leatherbacks enjoy a diet of jellyfish; hawksbills use their sharp beaks to snap up sea sponges. Green turtles eat sea grasses, whereas other sea turtles feed on crabs, insects, and algae[4] [ăl´ jē].

---

[3] marine: of or relating to the sea
[4] algae: a large group of plants that have no roots, stems, or leaves; seaweed is one type of algae

6   Turtles can live very long lives. In fact, some kinds of turtles live as long as 150 years. Several kinds have lifespans of about 50 years.

Mysteries of Turtle Life

7   Sea turtles are difficult creatures to study because they spend most of their lives at sea. After hatching from eggs laid on beaches, young turtles immediately head for the water. Females return

Thousands of olive ridley turtles have come to a beach in Costa Rica to lay their eggs. Though millions of eggs will be laid, only a few hatchlings will survive to adulthood.

to the same sandy beach only to lay eggs, and most males never return to land at all.

8   Where do these turtles travel during their long lives? In the 1950s, scientists began putting small metal tags on sea turtles and then releasing the animals into the sea. Later, when scientists in another part of the world recovered these same turtles, they could tell where the animals had come from and how far they had traveled. In the 1980s, scientists attached radio transmitters[5] to large sea turtles so that satellites could track the turtles' movements.

9   The latest way to track sea turtles is to study the blood of turtles recovered around the world. Scientists have discovered that turtles from different beaches have different gene[6] patterns, which show up in their blood. A turtle's blood can reveal where that turtle was born. Blood studies have shown that sea turtles often swim thousands of miles from their birthplaces. For example, researchers now know that sea turtles found in Greece swam there from the United States. Most sea turtles recovered off the coast of California were born on a beach in Japan. These turtles had made an amazing journey of 7,500 miles!

---

[5] radio transmitter: a device that sends out signals
[6] gene: a tiny unit of a plant or animal cell that determines characteristics that are passed on from one generation to the next

After hatching, baby turtles race seaward. Even after escaping the dangers of the land, they face growing peril in the water from the fishing industry.

Danger!

10 It seems that just when we are starting to understand sea turtles, we may be losing them. If steps are not taken soon, they may die out entirely. The situation of the Kemp's ridley turtle is the most desperate. There are only about a thousand nesting pairs left in the world. But they are not the only sea turtles in danger. All types of sea turtles are having trouble surviving in the modern world.

11 During their long migrations[7] [mī grā´shənz], sea turtles face danger from humans. Fishing

---

[7] migration: movement from one place to another, especially at certain times of the year

boats drop what are known as *longlines,* very long fishing lines studded with fishhooks. A longline might be 75 miles long and have thousands of hooks. The lines are meant to catch tuna and other fish, but unsuspecting turtles often become trapped in them too. Captured turtles cannot reach the surface of the water to take in air, and without air, the turtles drown. Thousands of turtles die in this way each year.

12   Shrimp fishing also kills sea turtles by the thousands. To catch as many shrimp as possible, shrimp boats drag nets behind them. Along with shrimp, they scoop up fish, turtles, and every other sea animal unlucky enough to be in their way. Laws say that shrimp nets must have turtle escape hatches. However, some shrimpers tie the hatches shut to protect their catch, dooming the sea turtles to death.

13   In addition to the dangers from longlines and shrimp nets, there are several other reasons that sea turtles are in trouble. Some turtles, such as hawksbills, are hunted for their beautiful shells. In Japan, hawksbill shells are highly prized and sell for more than $300 apiece. The shells are made into combs, earrings, tie clips, and bowls.

14   Some adult sea turtles are killed for food. For example, green turtle soup is a special dish that is served around the world. The meat of adult sea turtles is used to make green turtle soup. Sea turtle eggs are another popular delicacy. People

in Mexico and Costa Rica comb the beaches to find the eggs and then eat them raw.

15   Finally, the appeal of oceanfront land is making sea turtle populations plunge. Resort hotels are being built on beaches that sea turtles have long used for nesting. Now, when turtles arrive to scoop out nests and lay eggs, they find the sand dotted with hotels and people. Curious hotel guests often move or damage the eggs. Even after some turtles are able to hatch, they can become confused by the lights coming from the hotels. They crawl toward the lights and away from the ocean and become easy prey for raccoons.

Some people consider these sea turtle eggs fine food.

Sea turtles such as this hawksbill are protected by the U.S. government. Individual citizens can also find out what they can do to help sea turtles survive.

What Does the Future Hold?

16   There is hope. Scientists are doing what they can to help sea turtles. Each year, thousands of baby turtles are gathered from beaches. These babies are put into special nurseries. When they are bigger and stronger, they are set free again. At that point, they have a better chance of living to adulthood.

17   Other steps are being taken as well. Some beaches are now set aside for nesting turtles. In

some places the gathering of turtle eggs has been outlawed or limited.

18   Still, sea turtles face a shaky future. Most experts say that saving the sea turtle will require cooperation among nations. After all, these animals cannot tell where one country's waters end and another's begin. The international community must agree on rules to protect these ancient and beautiful creatures—before it is too late.

QUESTIONS

1. What is the largest kind of sea turtle, and about how much can it weigh?
2. Why do scientists find it difficult to study sea turtles?
3. How are longlines and shrimp nets dangerous for sea turtles?
4. How does the development of oceanfront land lessen the sea turtle's chances of survival?
5. What efforts are being made to protect sea turtles?

Modern archaeologists are excited about the discovery in China of an army of clay soldiers buried more than 2,000 years ago.

A
Silent Army
of Clay

*Why was a vast clay army buried near the grave
of the first emperor of China?*

1   The year was 1974. It was an ordinary day in the
Chinese countryside. Farmers were hard at work
digging a new well. One digger was surprised
when his shovel hit a piece of hard terra-cotta[1]
clay. When he pulled out the clay piece, he
discovered that it was the head of a statue. More
digging revealed the rest of the life-sized statue
of an ancient Chinese warrior dressed for battle.
The farmers did not find the water they were
looking for. Instead they discovered what is
thought to be the most important archaeological
[är kē ə lŏj´ĭ kəl] find of the 20th century.

2   The farmers were eager to share their find, so
they reported it to local authorities. Excited
archaeologists [är kē ŏl´ə jĭsts] came to the site

---

[1] terra-cotta: a brownish red fired clay used for statues,
pottery, and decorations

and started digging. They knew that the site was close to the ancient tomb of the first emperor of China, Qin Shihuangdi [chĭn shē hwäng dē´]. Was this statue the only one of its kind, or were there more like it? Could this statue be connected in some way to the emperor's tomb? The answers soon became clear as statue after statue was uncovered. Experts decided that the statues were part of a silent army put in place to defend the emperor after his death. Incredibly, nearly 7,500 clay soldiers dressed for battle have been uncovered.

By conquering rival kingdoms, Qin Shihuangdi became the first emperor of China.

Who Was Qin Shihuangdi?

3   Who was this man who needed an army to guard him in death? Qin Shihuangdi is considered one of the most important leaders in Chinese history. The Qin dynasty lasted less than 40 years, but it shaped China in many important ways.

4   Ying Zheng was only 13 years old when he became the king of Qin in 246 B.C. At that time, China was divided into seven separate kingdoms that warred with each other constantly. Ying quickly grew into a powerful and brutal leader. He battled the other states for about nine years, during which time more than a million people were killed. The Qin kingdom finally conquered all of the six other kingdoms. As leader of all of the states, Ying Zheng gave himself a new name—Qin Shihuangdi, meaning "First Emperor of Qin."

Qin Shihuangdi's Accomplishments

5   Once Qin had all the states under his control, he began sweeping changes to ensure that the new empire would run smoothly. He created a central government and designated [dĕz´ĭg nāt əd] an official language and writing system. He decreed that everyone should use the same coins, round metal coins with a square hole in the middle. Under his rule, weights and

measures were standardized.² He also
established a new set of laws.

6   Qin Shihuangdi showed his power with
huge building projects. His people worked on
the Great Wall of China, making it strong and
unbroken for thousands of miles. They built
more than 700 palaces for him in all parts of
the empire. Workers leveled hills and valleys to
build wide, straight roads around the empire.
The emperor and his armies could travel these
roads quickly to put down revolts³ anywhere in
the empire.

The Dark Side of the Qin Empire

7 Qin was able to accomplish so much because
he had complete control of his people. He did
not allow anyone to question his authority in
any way. At one point, his own scholars
recommended that China go back to the old
ways of governing. Qin became enraged that
they would compare his rule with what he
considered the mistakes of the past. He decreed
that all historical records be destroyed. Later,
when 460 of his advisors criticized his policies,
he had them all buried alive.

---

² standardized: made the same; brought in line with a
particular standard or rule
³ revolt: a rebellion; a rising up of the people against a
government or authority

8   Qin made sure everyone followed his new laws. Anyone who refused to obey him was punished severely or put to death. Those found guilty of breaking even the least important law were sentenced to forced labor.

Fear of Death

9   It is easy to understand why Qin felt that he was in danger from both his enemies and his own people. From an early age he was obsessed[4] with finding a way to avoid death. He was sure that there must be a potion that would help him live forever. Traveling

Every warrior's face shows a different personality.

around his empire, he searched for the magical substance that would give him immortality.[5]

10   At the same time that he sought the potion of life, Qin prepared for his death. Soon after becoming king of Qin, he started work on his tomb. At one point he had 700,000 people working on the construction of the most amazing

---

[4] obsessed: unable to stop thinking about a certain topic
[5] immortality: life without end

tomb possible. Skilled craftsmen worked for more than 36 years to build the tomb and the army of clay soldiers that would protect it for eternity.

11   In spite of all his efforts to find eternal life, Qin died at the age of 49. The Qin empire wanted to keep the contents of the tomb a secret, so all of the artists and laborers who worked on it were shut inside and buried alive along with the emperor.

Archaeologists are working with great care to uncover and repair the figures buried near the tomb of Qin Shihuangdi.

The Terra-cotta Army

12 Qin believed that he would need all the comforts of life in the afterlife. Since his empire had been built on military might, he assumed that he would need an army in the next life. So he had workers build an army from clay.

13   Though made of clay more than 2,000 years ago, these warriors look real and alive. Many of them carry weapons of the time, such as bronze swords, spears, battle-axes, and crossbows. Full-size horses pull chariots; officers, soldiers, and guards stand ready for battle. Some soldiers wear armor; others wear clothing that matches their rank and position in the army. Bits of color show that the soldiers were once painted in bright colors.

14   The soldiers are grouped in three pits. The first pit contains nearly 6,000 foot soldiers and archers. The smaller second pit contains 1,400 figures including chariot drivers, the cavalry, and horses. There are also 90 wooden chariots in this pit. A third pit contains about 70 figures that represent the officers.

15   The figures are quite tall. Most of the soldiers are 5 feet, 11 inches tall. The archers are about 6 feet tall, and the officers are even taller. One officer is 6 feet, 7 inches tall, probably taller than any officer in Qin's army really was. Their bodies, arms, and legs may have been made in large numbers using the same molds, and they were probably put together by hand.

16   The soldiers are impressive indeed, standing at attention in row after row. Perhaps the most incredible thing about the terra-cotta army is their faces. No two faces are exactly the same. They differ in shape, features, and expressions. Some soldiers look ferocious, while others seem thoughtful. Some are serious, while others seem good natured. Experts have guessed that the faces of the soldiers may be the faces of those who created them. Craftsmen may have copied the faces of the workers that surrounded them. No one knows for sure why they are different.

Archaeologists at Work

17   Archaeologists are working hard to re-create the terra-cotta army. China has built a museum above the work site to protect the soldiers from the wind and rain while workers uncover them. Many figures have broken apart and must be carefully put back together. Workers are also reassembling the horses, chariots, and weapons. Those who have visited the site report that while each figure is a marvel in itself, seeing thousands of them standing in one place is breathtaking. Many people consider this still and silent army the eighth wonder of the world.

18   Slowly, archaeologists are making their way to the tomb itself. They have not uncovered the burial site yet, but they are excited about what

they might find there someday. According to legend, the tomb is filled with treasures and jewels. Old stories say that workers dug rivers and filled them with mercury,[6] and that the mercury is made to flow in some unknown way. They also say that there are stars and planets on the ceiling and mountains and canyons on the floor. Who knows what other wonders await? ◆

QUESTIONS

1. What were the terra-cotta soldiers supposed to guard?
2. What changes did Qin Shihuangdi make to help China run smoothly?
3. How did Qin Shihuangdi punish those who disobeyed or criticized him?
4. What is remarkable about the faces of the clay soldiers?
5. Why were the artists and craftsmen who worked on the terra-cotta army buried alive?

_____

[6] mercury: a heavy silver-white metallic element that is liquid at normal temperatures

For thousands of years, lighthouses have led sailors to safe harbors. The North Head Lighthouse on the Washington coast shines its light over the Pacific Ocean.

Lighthouses
Sentinels by the Sea

How have lighthouses helped sailors for centuries?

1　As long as people have loved adventure, they have braved the open seas. With only small, fragile boats to protect them, mariners[1] [măr´ ĭ nərz] of long ago set out to explore and to trade. And ever since mariners began traveling across oceans and lakes, they have faced danger. But if they were lucky, before trouble hit they would see the welcome beam of a lighthouse. Its light would guide them home.

2　A lighthouse fills two important needs: It tells mariners where they are and it warns them that they are near dangerous areas.

---

[1] mariner: a sailor

The Point Bonita Lighthouse in San Francisco uses a lens developed by engineer Augustin-Jean Fresnel in 1822.

Without lighthouses to guide them, countless ships have been wrecked on hidden rocks and underwater shoals.[2]

Lighthouses of Long Ago

3 Lighthouses have been around for thousands of years in one form or another. Perhaps the first lights to guide sailors home were large bonfires on the shore. Ancient peoples probably built these fires, hoping their seafaring friends would spot them and return safely. People soon learned

───────────────

[2] shoal: a shallow place in a body of water

that if they raised the fires as high as possible, sailors could see the light better and from farther away. So they sometimes built the fires on elevated platforms.

4   Perhaps the most famous lighthouse of ancient times was the Pharos, the lighthouse at Alexandria, Egypt. Much more sophisticated than a platform topped with a bonfire, this lighthouse was huge, about as high as a 40-story building. At its base was a marble, block-square building. On top of that was a tower; on top of that, a cylinder;[3] and on top of that, a huge fire and a mirror. The mirror reflected the light and made it stronger. It was said that ships as far as 35 miles away could see the light at night.

From Candles to Electricity

5 People eventually decided that fires were not the best source of light for lighthouses. Much of the light from fires is wasted because it goes up into the air instead of out to sea. In addition, huge fires need to be tended constantly, and they are dangerous. People began to look for new ways to make light. They hit upon the idea of lighting many candles in lanterns and placing the lanterns on a raised platform. Then they began burning whale oil, kerosene, and even lard in the lanterns.

---

[3] cylinder: a solid object whose ends are equal and parallel circles

6   Clearly, lanterns or candles don't give enough light to guide mariners far at sea. Inventors searched for a better way to create a strong light. In 1815 an engineer named Augustin-Jean Fresnel [frā nĕl´] developed a lens that changed lighthouses forever. Surrounding the lantern with a series of cut-glass rings and prisms,[4] the Fresnel lens reflected and magnified the light. It sent a powerful beam over the water.

7   Lighthouses used a combination of the Fresnel lens and lanterns well into the 20th century. Since many lighthouses were built in isolated areas of the coast, it took many years for electric lines to reach them. Wherever electricity was not available, the lighthouse keeper lit the flame at night and made sure it stayed lit until morning.

Building a Better Tower

8   Just as important as the lighthouse light is the tower from which it shines. The early lighthouses were all built on land. Even though ships often ran into trouble on offshore rocks, people thought it was impossible to build a lighthouse near a dangerous area. In 1695 a talented builder named Harry

---

[4] prism: a transparent body made of glass or plastic, whose ends are parallel triangles; used for breaking up light rays

This painting shows the third lighthouse built on the Eddystone rocks. It stood there for 127 years.

Winstanley took on the task of building an offshore lighthouse. He chose a spot where many shipwrecks had taken place—the Eddystone rocks in England.

9   Building the lighthouse took years. Only when the weather was good could the crew row the 14 miles to the building site. On bad days, waves would wash over the site and sometimes undo what had been done the day before. When the lighthouse finally opened, it became a tourist attraction. Winstanley's Eddystone light operated for only five years before it was destroyed by a

huge storm. A second and then a third light were built; each was destroyed. Today a fourth Eddystone light stands on the site.

10   The first Eddystone light was a fancy circular tower. Other towers are cones, pyramids, skeletons, or blocks. Towers can be made of brick, stone, wood, and metal. Part of the fun of visiting lighthouses is seeing how each tower is different from others.

Making Each Lighthouse Different

11   Lighthouses are made different on purpose. Remember that a major function of a lighthouse is to help mariners figure out where they are. For that reason, each lighthouse has special characteristics to make it different from the others around it.

12   For example, one lighthouse may have a light that flashes white and then red. The next lighthouse may repeat a special sequence: flash a light once, then twice, then three times; again,

The lighthouse at Cape Hatteras, North Carolina, is painted in a distinctive pattern.

once, then twice, then three times. Still another lighthouse may have a 10-second period of darkness followed by a three-second period of light. At another location, there may be two or even three lighthouses, not just one. Mariners check a light list that tells which way each light shines.

13   Lighthouses also help mariners pinpoint their locations during the day. This is why lighthouses are painted in different colors and designs. For example, the lighthouse at Cape Hatteras, on the North Carolina coast, has diagonal, black-and-white stripes to set it apart from others nearby.

Lighthouses Today

14   Modern mariners do not depend on lighthouses as much as sailors of the past did. Technology such as radar[5] and the Global Positioning System helps mariners pinpoint their locations more accurately than ever before. Also, in places where lights may be helpful, it is easier to use a plastic light on a pole or on a buoy to do the job. For keepers to devote their lives to taking care of lighthouses that are unnecessary and expensive is seen as a waste of time and money. For these reasons, most lighthouses have been closed and abandoned. Vandals have destroyed the lights and the

---

[5] radar: a device or system that uses radio waves to locate objects

towers of some, and the sea threatens to pull down others.

15   Many people do not want to see these old lighthouses ruined. For several years, they have been buying them and putting them to new uses. Some have become museums that explain the lives of lighthouse keepers and their families, as well as the history of the individual lighthouse. Others have become inns or bed-and-breakfasts.[6] Organizations to preserve lighthouses have sprung up and are raising money to save these symbols of the past.

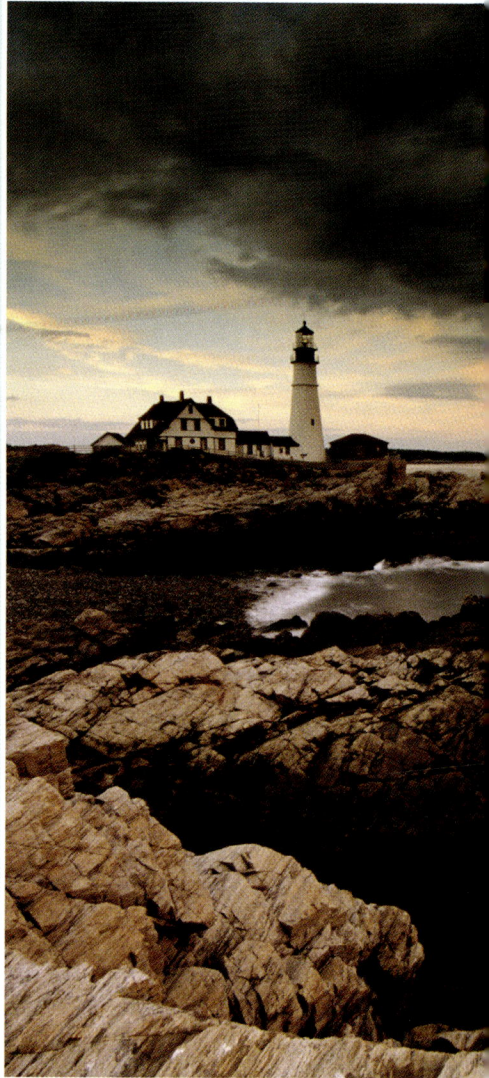

---

[6] bed-and-breakfast: an overnight lodging that provides travelers both a place to sleep and a breakfast in the morning

16   Even though the lighthouse may have lost its usefulness, it is still a well-loved symbol. To some people, it represents a quieter time—one before radios, telephones, television, and computers. In a world that sometimes seems not to care, it stands for our willingness to help each other in times of trouble. ◆

QUESTIONS

1. What are the two main purposes of lighthouses?
2. Why did the Egyptians build the Pharos lighthouse so tall?
3. How did the Fresnel lens improve the way lighthouses worked?
4. Name two ways in which lighthouses were made different from each other.
5. Why have most lighthouses become unnecessary today?

Blame It on

Poltergeists

Are poltergeists to blame when things go bump in the night?

1 Eleven-year-old Virginia Campbell was staying with her aunt and uncle while her father was away on a business trip. On November 22, 1960, Virginia climbed into bed with her nine-year-old cousin, Margaret, ready for a quiet night of sleep. But the night was not going to be quiet or ordinary. In fact, Virginia's life was not going to be the same for many days.

2 Soon after the lights went out that night, both girls heard a loud thump, like the sound of a ball bouncing near their bed. The girls got up and searched the room, but the thumping continued.

Some people believe in poltergeists. These rowdy spirits were probably blamed for the rocks mysteriously thrown at windows in a house in France in 1849.

Frightened, they ran downstairs to Mr. and Mrs. Campbell. The noise followed them and continued while the adults searched in vain for its source. The tired girls finally went back to bed. The noise continued until Virginia fell asleep.

3   The next day, more strange things happened. As Virginia sat in the living room with her aunt and uncle, a heavy wooden table moved several inches away from the wall and then back. Everyone was shocked. That night, the thumping sound started again. This time the noise was louder and more insistent.[1] It was a long time before Virginia could get to sleep.

4   Over the next several days, the Campbell family witnessed odd movements of furniture around their house. They heard unexplained knocking, tapping, and pounding. Neighbors were called in to verify that these events were indeed happening and that Virginia could not have been behind them. It did seem suspicious, however, that she was always around when they happened.

5   The weird occurrences even followed Virginia to school. There, her desk kept opening and closing, in spite of her efforts to keep it shut. Even the desk behind hers rose into the air. When Virginia stood by the teacher's desk, it began to vibrate so violently that the pointer rolled off of it.

---

[1] insistent: demanding attention; going on and on

6   Virginia and the Campbells were becoming more and more upset. They feared it was only a matter of time until someone got hurt. Everyone, including Virginia, was relieved when her father came back from his business trip on December 1. After he took his daughter home, the strange events stopped as suddenly as they had started.

A ghost hunter tests for poltergeist activity. He is drawing a chalk outline around a vase to see if spirits move the vase.

Noisy Ghosts

7 What could have caused the loud noises and the furniture that moved by itself? Some people believe that Virginia was the victim of a poltergeist. *Poltergeist* [pōl´tər gīst] is a German word meaning "noisy ghost." Unlike other, better-behaved ghosts, poltergeists are not misty shapes that politely appear and then silently fade away. Poltergeists are loud and mischievous [mĭs´chə vəs]. You know they are around when you hear, feel, or see the tricks they do.

Was it Esther Cox or a poltergeist who set fires around this house in Amherst, Nova Scotia?

8 The antics[2] of poltergeists have been reported all around the world for centuries. Witnesses say poltergeists have done all of the following: made strange noises, moved household objects, thrown stones, and caused liquids to ooze from walls. According to believers, poltergeists have set fires, caused static on radios, disrupted phone conversations, turned lights on and off, and, in

---

[2] antic: a playful or silly action

general, made nuisances of themselves.

9   Poltergeists don't haunt certain places, as other ghosts are said to do. Instead, they stick close to certain people. The focus, the poltergeist's victim, cannot escape by going to another place. The poltergeist simply follows that person to the new location. The focus is usually a young person under the age of 20. In most cases, the focus is a teen-aged girl who is having some kind of personal problem.

10   Usually, poltergeist stories are not too scary. After all, hearing a strange noise at night can be unnerving, but it isn't harmful. However, poltergeists have been blamed for more serious hauntings. For example, in the case of the Amherst, Nova Scotia, Poltergeist, a young woman named Esther Cox became seriously ill as a result of ghostly activity. Several fires were started around her, and she was blamed for them. She even spent time in jail for starting the blazes.

Possible Explanations

11 Is it possible that any of these stories about poltergeists are true? Many people swear that they have seen, heard, and felt poltergeists in action. They firmly believe that poltergeists do exist. But even those who study paranormal[3] events cannot agree about what exactly a poltergeist is, if it does exist. Several possible explanations have been put forward. See if any of these make sense to you.

- Poltergeists are spirits that are always around but have no power in this world. When they sense energy coming from an anxious or sad teenager, they zero in on him or her. Through the young person, they enter our world.

- The energy of a young person can actually create a poltergeist. Poltergeists cannot exist without that person's energy.

- A poltergeist is an unrecognized part of the focus's personality. According to this theory, everyone has a conscious,[4] known personality. He or she also has a hidden, unknown personality that becomes powerful in times of stress. This personality has the ability to influence its surroundings in surprising ways. For example, it uses psychokineses [sī´kō kĭ nē´sĭs], the ability to move objects without touching them.

---

[3] paranormal: not normal; not having a scientific explanation
[4] conscious: awake; aware

- Reports of poltergeists are simply stories made up by young people hungry for attention. Every trick a "poltergeist" does can be explained by a trained observer or a good magician.

Poltergeist or Fake?

12   Certainly, there is evidence to support the last explanation. For example, in 1984, the Resch family of Columbus, Ohio, reported odd occurrences that many people thought were the work of a poltergeist. Lights were going on and off in the Resch home, and objects were flying

Tina Resch reacts to a floating telephone, seemingly the work of a poltergeist.

through the air. It seemed that all of these events took place near their daughter, Tina. The Resches called a newspaper reporter, who came to their home with a photographer.

13   The Resches and their guests saw a loveseat move, a tissue box fly toward Tina, and a rug land on Tina's head. The photographer even snapped a picture of a phone flying in front of a terrified Tina. TV crews and other reporters came running to find out more.

14   Again the poltergeist struck. When no one was looking, a lamp crashed to the ground. But this time, Tina had made a mistake. A cameraman who had walked away had left the tape running and caught the accident on film. When played in slow motion, the tape revealed that Tina pulled the lamp down herself and then stood up and screamed in surprise.

15   Later, Tina admitted to the trick. But she insisted that she really was haunted by poltergeists and that everything else she had claimed was true. After that one trick, however, it was hard to believe her. And yet, how could a young girl have staged the other events so skillfully?

16   Experts, believers, skeptics,[5] and the general public will never agree whether poltergeists exist. If a person wants to believe, there is

---

[5] skeptic: a person who doubts that something is true

plenty of evidence to support that belief. If a person can't accept such an unlikely story, no amount of so-called evidence will convince him or her. Whether they want to or not, believers and skeptics will have to agree to disagree about poltergeists. ◆

QUESTIONS

1. Who is the most likely focus of a poltergeist's tricks?
2. Describe a few tricks that poltergeists are supposed to have played.
3. How are ghosts and poltergeists different?
4. Why do some people doubt whether Tina Resch was really haunted by poltergeists?
5. Why do some people still believe that Tina was bothered by poltergeists?

The
Last Queen
of *Hawaii*

Which is stronger, a kingdom or a song?

1 Say "Hawaii" to non-Hawaiians and most of them
will think of palm trees and necklaces made of
flowers. They will imagine feeling a warm sun and
pleasant breeze. And they will think of Hawaii's
most famous song, "Aloha Oe" [ä lō´ hä ō ā´]. This
song has come to stand for Hawaii around the
world. Yet few of the millions who can hum it know
that it was written by the last queen of Hawaii.

From "Lydia" to "Liliuokalani"

2 The queen-to-be was born in 1838, the third of
10 children. She was named Lydia. Both her
father and mother were chiefs. When she was
four years old, Lydia was sent to a school run by
missionaries. The school was strange to her at
first. Lydia had spoken only Hawaiian at home.
Now she had to learn English. But she quickly

**Queen Liliuokalani (1838–1917) poses for an official portrait.
A brave and talented woman, she ruled Hawaii for barely two
years, from 1891 to 1893.**

learned to speak and write well in her second language. She later said, "I was a studious girl; and the acquisition[1] of knowledge has been a passion with me during my whole life."

3   Another passion was music. She sang, learned to play the piano, and began to write songs. Eventually she would publish over 160 songs, including one of Hawaii's four national anthems.

4   After she left school, Lydia joined the social life of the court[2] of the Hawaiian king. In 1862 she married a childhood friend, John Dominis. Dominis was the son of a Boston sea captain. His father had been lost at sea 20 years before, just after building a fine home in Honolulu [hōn´ə lōō´lōō]. His mother had held onto the home by renting out rooms. One renter told so many stories about George Washington that people called the house Washington Place. After their wedding, Lydia and John moved in with John's mother at Washington Place.

5   In 1874 Lydia's brother David Kalakaua [kä lä´kou wä] was chosen by the Hawaiian legislature[3] to become the new king. Three years

---

[1] acquisition: the process of acquiring, that is, gaining by one's own actions

[2] court: the family, advisors, and others who serve a king or ruler

[3] legislature: a group of people that makes and passes the laws for a country or state

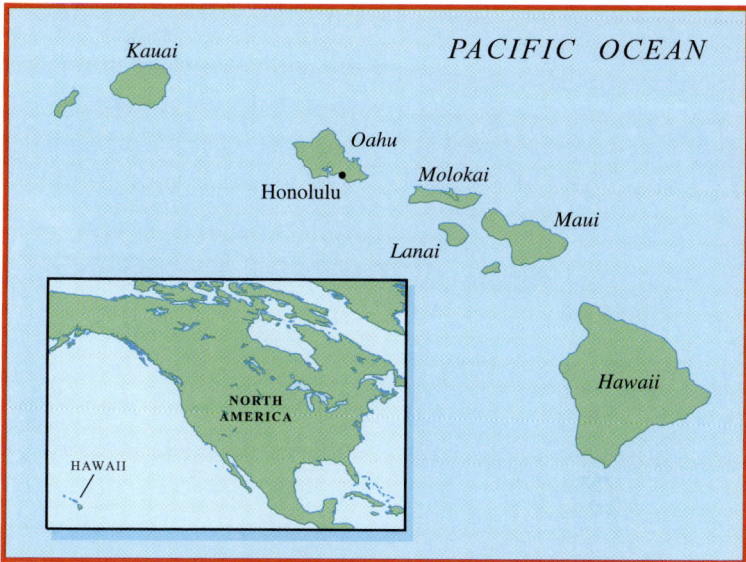

Hawaii is an island chain 2,400 miles southwest of the U.S. mainland. Most of its people live on the largest islands.

later King Kalakaua announced that Lydia would take the throne when he died. After that, Lydia always used her royal name, Liliuokalani [lē lē´ o͞o ō kä lä´ nē].

6   In many ways, being heir to the throne did not change Liliuokalani's life. She still enjoyed riding horses, visiting friends, and playing the piano. It was during this time that she composed her most famous song. In 1878, she and several friends and servants rode from Honolulu to another friend's home near a beautiful bay. As they started back, the princess noticed one of the young men in her group sadly leaving a girl from the area. Soon she started to hum a tune and put together a poem

This flower wreath includes portraits of some of Hawaii's royalty. Queen Liliuokalani is pictured in the center on the right.

about the parting of lovers. When she got back to Washington Place, she wrote the words and music to "Aloha Oe." The title means "farewell to you." The verses of the song are all in Hawaiian, but the chorus (the part that repeats after each verse) combines Hawaiian with the English words "one fond embrace . . . until we meet again."

7   As heir to the throne, Liliuokalani now had public duties. She took part in civic events, such as the ceremony that began work on the first railroad on Kauai [kou´wä ē]. The princess herself drove the first spike. She showed concern for her people by visiting those in need. For example, she visited the leper colony on Molokai [mō lō kä´ē]. Whenever King Kalakaua left the country for a long time, Liliuokalani ruled in his place.

8   Liliuokalani also represented the king in foreign countries. In 1887, for example, she traveled with Kalakaua's wife, Queen Kapiolani [kä pē´ ō lä´ nē]. They visited Washington, D.C., on their way to England. There, the two royal

Hawaiians joined the English court to celebrate Queen Victoria's Diamond Jubilee. This event marked Victoria's 50 years as queen of England.

9   While Liliuokalani was on this trip, something awful happened in Hawaii. King Kalakaua had been trying to limit the power of the rich landowners from other countries, many of them from the United States. The foreigners joined forces and threatened the king. Fearing for his life, Kalakaua signed a constitution[4] in which he gave up all real power. This new law of the land took the vote from most native Hawaiians. It gave the vote to settlers from the United States and Europe instead.

10   When King Kalakaua died in January 1891, Liliuokalani became queen. Just seven months later, her husband died. Since they had no children, the queen named her 16-year-old niece Kaiulani [kä yōō´ lä nē] as her heir.

Four Days That Ended a Kingdom

11   Queen Liliuokalani's greatest wish was to get rid of the Constitution of 1887. For two years she worked secretly to write a new constitution. This law would return power to her people. On January 14, 1893, she was ready to announce her constitution.

---

[4] constitution: the central law or set of laws by which a country or state is governed

12   But her enemies heard of her plans and decided to revolt, or rise up against her government. A U.S. warship happened to be in Honolulu Harbor. The revolutionaries[5] sent a letter to the U.S. minister to Hawaii, John L. Stevens. They falsely claimed that their lives were in danger. To help them, Stevens ordered armed troops from the warship ashore. The troops took up posts around the palace, trapping the queen.

13   On January 17, the revolutionaries declared that they had taken over the country. A temporary government would rule, they said, until the United States annexed (took over) Hawaii. With U.S. soldiers posted around her, Liliuokalani surrendered. She was sure that when the U.S. government heard the whole story, she would be returned to power. Meanwhile, she left the palace and went to Washington Place.

14   Young Princess Kaiulani went to Washington, D.C. She persuaded President Grover Cleveland to investigate the matter. Cleveland became convinced that Minister Stevens had misused his power. He said Liliuokalani should be returned to the throne.

15   Those who had taken power from the queen refused to give it up. Instead, in 1894 they formed the Republic of Hawaii. Most native

[5] revolutionary: a person who takes part in a revolution (the overthrow of a government)

Queen Liliuokalani returned to Washington Place after revolutionaries took over the country.

Hawaiians supported the queen. They wanted Liliuokalani back as their ruler. The next January, Liliuokalani's supporters revolted against the Republic. They were defeated after 10 days of fighting, and many were arrested. When guns were found in the garden of Washington Place, Liliuokalani, too, was arrested.

16   The queen was led to believe that if she resigned, the other prisoners would be released. To save them, she signed a statement giving up the throne. Still the prisoners were not released. Many were given long prison terms. Four were

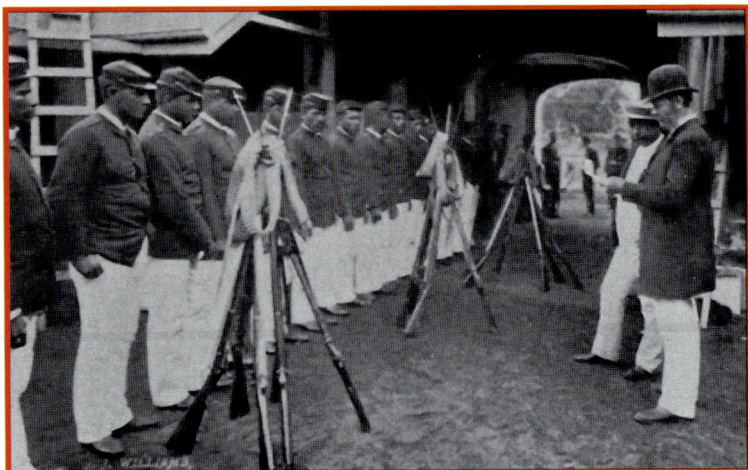

On January 17, 1893, U.S. troops stand in formation outside the Queen's palace, marking the end of the Hawaiian government.

sentenced to death. The queen herself was sentenced to a fine of $5,000 and five years of hard labor in prison.

17   For eight months Liliuokalani was held in one room of the palace. She was not allowed to have visitors, and only one servant was allowed to be with her. Then, on January 1, 1896, all of the prisoners were freed—all but the queen. She was arrested and not allowed to leave the palace until late in the year.

18   As soon as she was free, Liliuokalani went to Washington, D.C., to talk with President Cleveland. He was sympathetic but could do nothing. Two years later, when William McKinley was president, the Spanish-American War started.

The United States needed a naval[6] base in the Pacific Ocean. The Republic of Hawaii once more asked to be annexed. This time the United States agreed. The queen refused to watch as the U.S. flag was raised over her former palace.

19   Liliuokalani kept the Hawaiian flag flying over Washington Place, where she lived for the rest of her life. She never gave up fighting for the rights of Hawaiians. Her people honored her as their queen until her death at the age of 79, in 1917.

20   During her brief time as queen, Liliuokalani was a symbol of her country. Now, more than 100 years after the end of her reign, her song is a lasting symbol of Hawaii.

QUESTIONS
1. What is "Aloha Oe"?
2. In what art did Liliuokalani have talent?
3. What were some of Liliuokalani's duties after her brother named her his heir?
4. Why did Queen Liliuokalani want to get rid of the Constitution of 1887?
5. What happened when the queen's supporters tried to put her back on the throne?

---

[6] naval: having to do with a navy

PHOTO CREDITS

Cover Jerry Alexander/Stone. **vi** CORBIS. **3** The New-York Historical Society. **4** Stock Montage. **7** CORBIS. **10** Kevin Horan/Stone. **13** PhotoDisc. **14** Bettmann/CORBIS. **15** Paul A. Souders/CORBIS. **17** Paul A. Souders/CORBIS. **20** Hulton/Archive. **23** (c) 1997 by National Geographic Society. All Rights Reserved. **24** Alfred Eisenstaedt/TimePix. **27** Paul Damien/Stone. **28** PhotoDisc. **30** Museum of the City of New York/CORBIS. **33, 34** Bureau of Engraving and Printing. **37** The United States Mint. **40** Kevin Schafer/Stone. **43** Juan Carlos Ulate/Reuters/Archive Photos. **45** Peter Weinmann/Animals Animals. **47** Gerrard Lacz/Animals Animals. **50** An Keren/Photo Researchers. **52** The Art Archive/British Library. **55** Glen Allison/Stone. **56** An Keren/PPS/Photo Researchers. **60** Michael T. Sedam/CORBIS. **62** James A. Sugar/CORBIS. **65** Mary Evans Picture Library. **66** Randy Wells/Stone. **70** Mary Evans Picture Library. **73** Kurt Hutton/Hulton Getty/Archive. **74** Mary Evans Picture Library. **77** Mansell/Timepix. **80** Bettmann/Corbis. **84** Mansell/Timepix. **87** Hawaii State Archives. **88** Library of Congress.